Looking, Seeing

Looking, Seeing

© 2018

by Chris Pepple

cover art by

Eryn "Kat" Pepple

To all of you who have walked with
me on this journey,
thank you…

Because I have been loved,
I hope to love…
Because I have been seen,
I hope to see…
Because I have been heard,
I hope to hear…

No parts of this book may be reproduced without explicit
permission from the author. Published 2018.
www.chrispepple.com

Preface

Finally, I am publishing as a poet. The first time I discovered my passion for writing, I wrote a poem. Somehow, though, I didn't feel like a poet (whatever that means), so I hid the poem away for years. I didn't know anyone who read poetry often, much less anyone who claimed to be a poet. I was scared of being judged. Don't we all fear that at times?

During my teen years, however, I still struggled to find my voice, to share with people what I was seeing on my journey through life. I didn't own a camera (well, eventually I owned a Polaroid), so I tried to capture what I saw and felt using my words to create the images. I saw farm workers and city employees, grandparents and aging aunts and uncles, young cousins, and new friends. I was a listener, so I heard them share their life stories. I saw them in their unique environments. And I heard gossip and rumors and jokes more than I wish to acknowledge.

As I moved around in Atlanta, in Memphis, and in Nashville, I remained a listener…I heard the stories of people from many faiths, from many walks of life, from many career fields, from many economic levels, and from many political groups. I never settled neatly into one place or with one single denomination or political party. I was just me, wandering through many perspectives and still listening.

I hope you discover and enjoy all of my quirks and complexities in this collection of poetry. I have tried to live my life in a way that allows me to truly see a wide diversity of the people who populate this wonderful world we all call home. I have also tried to listen and learn and grow along the way, hopefully bringing love along on the journey. As I grow, I have tried to honestly admit and learn from my own failures and weaknesses. I don't claim to be perfect (or even close to it).

Some of you who think you know me may be shocked at some of the poems. If you tried to neatly place me in your faith category or your political party or your social group, you may have assumed that in all areas of life I agreed with you. However, I hope you keep reading. I am a sum of all my parts, a student of all who opened their hearts and mentored me, a family member to all who accepted me, and a listener to all who trusted me with their stories. I am whole, yet I am also unique and complex like the pieces of stained glass that come together to form one window.

I can be a child of God and one who embraces diversity. I can be faithful and one who fights for social justice. I can be a quiet listener and a loud advocate. It's who I am as the whole, not fitting neatly into any predefined role that someone may wish me to fill. So here I am as the poet… enjoy the journey with me.

And, Readers, find your own voice in here. Bring your own images and stories to these readings. Ask what my words mean to me, but then claim them and make them your own. Let's join our voices together as we interpret and re-interpret the words and stories shared. Ask hard questions. Seek challenging answers. Move out of your comfort zone with some of these poems and find a shared familiar image through others.

We are uniquely created, but our lives are woven together in the fabric of our world that we call home. Our love and hopes and fears can be a place to start conversations that bring us closer together. Our scars can teach others about pain that comes from not being seen, not being heard, or not being believed—pain that comes through deep grief, and pain that comes from abuse from others. We are all scarred, yet we are all beautifully and wonderfully made. Let's all look to see the beauty in each life, the strengths of each person, the soul of the person you might have normally walked past. When we look, let's put aside our taught prejudices, set down our beliefs based on partial truths and rumors, and let go of our fears so we can truly see the gifts of the people we meet along our journeys.

I would like to end this beginning with two of my favorite quotes about poetry:

"… poetry is not a luxury. It is a vital necessity of our existence. It forms the quality of the light within which we predicate our hopes and dreams toward survival and change, first made into language, then into idea, then into more tangible action. Poetry is the way we help give name to the nameless so it can be thought." —Audre Lorde, *Sister Outsider*

"We don't read and write poetry because it's cute. We read and write poetry because we are members of the human race. And the human race is filled with passion. And medicine, law, business, engineering, these are noble pursuits and necessary to sustain life. But poetry, beauty, romance, love, these are what we stay alive for." —*Dead Poet Society*

discovering

me

Shredded Boxes

I shredded the box you tried to
place me in because I decided
I just couldn't fit in the confining,
defining space you offered some of us
to sit in, to wait in, to play in, because
as I sat in the box I began to dream
of all of the possibilities for my life
and I began to sketch pictures onto
the stiff brown walls that at first felt
so soothing and familiar, but then I
looked at the dreams I was fleshing
out on those walls and I wondered what
was outside of this box, this label,
this expectation of me…and I
wondered if my comfort was real
or if that, too, was defined by you,
so I raised my head above the folded
edges of the box, past the world you
had built for me and had told me I

was so very safe in and I saw
colors flying past not confined
to my sketches on the wall of the box
and I saw life dancing past and heard
the new rhythms of so many songs
and my faith asked me if I was scared
to step out of the box, and I almost said yes
because you told me that a life inside
the box was best, but I tasted the
sweetness of the milk and honey being
offered and I felt my legs ache to join the
dance, and you saw me and shamed me
for forsaking the gift of the box, but I
had already felt the pulse of the
heartbeat of the new life, the life of the free,
and I shredded the box and outside
I found me…

Beans on the Stove

Your Deep South kitchen fills my memories
as much as the scent of your meals on the stove
would fill my senses when I stepped off of
the hardwood floor of your dining room onto the
black and white linoleum in the place where you
worked your magic with the bounty of your garden.
If you're hungry now, there's beans on the stove,
you would laugh as you sensed my presence sneaking
nearer to your red metal table to steal a biscuit
left over from breakfast. That's all you can have now,
you said, and just one bowl or there won't be any
for the rest of us come suppertime.
I knew that some ham would be in the oven and
some fried pies would be waiting nearby and
soon the weather would have a chill in the air
and you would make your famous vegetable soup
with the tomatoes you canned last summer and
the last of the beans you pulled off the pole and
some corn from the field and carrots you told me
I had to eat and creamed potatoes would be in the

pot in your hands when you cooked up my
favorite meal and I would help roll out the dough
for dumplin's on your counter by the sink which
looked over your lilies when they bloomed
and when the back screen door creaked open
then slammed shut near dusk, you moved your
delicacies from the stove to the table, ready for your
hungry family to eat what my Nana's hands prepared.

By My Choices

The warrior rises up in me
weary but alive,
preparing for my boldest move,
but you do not recognize
my success
as you claim victory in
your demented mind—
for you see me as broken,
falling to the ground
defeated and branded
by your will…
but by my choice
I melted
freeing my spirit
to flow from your grip—
not snapped by your desires
but freed by my dreams,
spirit and breath
leaving your hands
to be molded again
by the hope inside of me,
by the gifts I still carry

untouched by your ways,
by the soul
that is freely moving
and finding new strength
rising up in me—
by my choice I melted free
flowing forever and
rediscovering me.

Water Marks

Just the other day
I walked down to the
lake and sat on the
edge and named
the ducks as they
swam past and they
talked with me about
their life and together
we laughed and I
got up to go and
noticed that I had
left tracks in the
mud through which I
tromped to find this
shore and I dreaded
the thought of retracing
my steps for the trek home
and I dreaded the thought
of home and I looked out

across the lake again and
I saw the rippling trail
teasing me with the
question of whether or not
I would follow
and I shed my shoes
and with undaunted hope
walked where I had never
been before and I looked
back to see that I had left
footprints across the water.

Just Me

I'm a cream-soda drinking,
chocolate-loving, veggie-eating
kind of woman…
I'm loud when I need to be,
but when I'm silent,
I still roar…
I don't cling to the toxic,
but toss it away
and I stay undefinable
in the world which
craves easily expressed normality…
I'm a jean-wearing, Nike-running,
nature-embracing, faith-walking,
dog-loving, cat-crazy,
gerbil-caring, snake-fearing,
back-trail hiking, state-park camping,
always tired single Mom
who wakes up early,
admires the arts,
and never makes my bed…
who loves my girls
and stays fiercely loyal to friends…

who loves to learn and tries to pray
and hates separating walls
and has seen the cruelty of AIDS
and the horror of abuse
and the pain caused
by diversity-fearing peers
who assume my whiteness
means I think like them.
Label me not by your
thoughts or your fears,
judge me not by a rumor
tossed carelessly around,
condemn me not solely
by a past action
which just means I failed
and I learned…
judge me not at all,
for your approval is
not what I seek,
but join me on this
winding journey
to discover the path that
leads to just me…

Inner Walls

I built a wall
to protect myself
from your words and your anger
and your rages and your lies
but the wall
closed me in from myself
and the breath I needed
to give life to my hopes and dreams
so I tore down the wall
and found a Spirit
wrapped around me like a shawl
that gave me life and breath
and strength to grow to reach
for the dreams I rediscovered
and this Spirit
blew away the rage
you tried to aim at me
and gave me the peace
I needed to deflect your words
and move past your anger
boiling over from your own soul…
You will not hinder

my journey any longer
or cause me again to fall
because I looked inside and
dug out all thoughts of you
and gave the power
you had held over me
back to myself
to not just survive,
but to thrive…

Lady-Like

Today while I was walking
down to the lake
I stopped along the
way to notice a
daffodil blooming by
an old rotting post
left from a fence
that my grandfather
built many years ago
and I remember that my
mother and grandmother
used to picnic by this fence
on warm spring days
as they took a break from
their toiling hours around
the farm and my grandmother
often brought me here, too,
when I was younger and I
remember climbing on the
fence only to hear my
grandmother wishing aloud

that I would get down
and when I finally obeyed
I would pick her a flower
and she would try not to smile
as she fussed over my
frolicking manner and warned
me that one day I would have to
start acting like a lady
even though I still have not
done that today but
I think of her as I climb
atop the remaining post and
smell the daffodil and forget
that I was on my way
to the lake.

Re-creation

Did you try
to define me
with your labels,
your agenda?
Did you try
to claim me
as yours?
Did it make you
feel powerful
to try to control
the thoughts
of another?
Did you feel
all-powerful
when you thought
you had re-created me
in your own image?

I heard your words
over my own,
I believed your lies
instead of my truths,
I lived your nightmares
and tossed out my dreams.

You controlled me,
but before you broke me
I found a whisper
of my voice,
a remnant of my truth,
a memory of my hopes.

Did you feel defeated
when I broke free?
Did you lose your identity
when you lost control of me?

I took back my life,
reclaimed my dreams,
and washed myself clean
of your handprints
on my soul.

I re-created my world
to bring back truth,
to find hope,
to include joy,
to redefine love
and to live it.
My re-created world
is filled with music
and laughter
that drown out
your voice
as you try to
lure me back into
the world
you think
you rule.
I painted over
the memories of you
and rewrote
the script for
my life.
Re-creation.
It's in my hands.
There is no you
in my plans.

A Comet's View

Comet, call me
from the sky…
Swing low for me
to catch a ride…
Take me from these endless days
of searching longingly
to know again
what I feel when I touch…
what I yearn for when I dream
Comet, call me
by my name
so I can hear it once again…
And I will dance with you across the sky
and meet myself again
on the other side

seeing

you

Seeing Around Corners

Look straight ahead and stay focused
on the plan, you said, but the plan
didn't include the faces just around the corner—
the ones working the underpaid jobs
that you said could join
the same journey I was on—
straight path to success, you said,
but you defined success as
amassed wealth and a plethora of possessions
that soon slowed my steps as
I started to settle on your plan and
declare myself there—
embraced by the ones I strived to please and
satisfied with my life as it was—comfortable—
but I kept catching glimpses of the ones
still just around the corner—
the woman bent over with the weight of fear—
the child pretending hunger wouldn't stop him—
the parent working a third job, earning
the leftover pay we tossed that way—
the addicted beggar trying to find answers—
the angry young student buying a gun—

the bullied girl hiding behind the playground slide—
the bleeding woman covering her scars—
and their pain made me want to turn away,
but I couldn't build walls high enough to ignore
what I had already seen, and I couldn't
congratulate myself and call my life complete
while I stayed true to your path of success,
so I learned to turn corners and to see
the faces I have learned to love
and the hands that reached out to hold mine
and the dances that moved through the streets
despite the pain behind the steps
and I redefined my success as tied
to their hope and our shared steps
and I learned that joy was not a gift
tied to the triumph I strived to reach
but was born just around the corners

LA Beauty

I stood behind you at the bus stop and saw
your tattered bag hanging by your side and
saw the coffee-colored designs on your shirt
that you had tried to wash away before you
left home and noticed the wear on your shoes
and wondered how many miles you
had walked in them as you trekked
back and forth on your daily tasks
and together we watched as the cars
rolled past with their drivers heading off
to fulfill another L.A. dream and we admired
their determination to keep the dream alive
because we knew that we had hopes
waiting to come alive and we thought
of our dreams as we waited there on the
curb in view of the Hollywood sign
and thought of the beauty in the
songs and the arts around us and
stepped back into our reality as we
boarded the bus with its musty smell
and wandering passengers and tired

faces and we sat on nearby rows and
looked at businesses and homes we moved past
and wondered about the lives of those around us
and then I realized the beauty in our journey
as you moved next to the man who others avoided
sitting near and you handed him your cup of coffee
knowing you would have no other for the day
and an older lady smiled at a young mother
holding a tired crying child and offered kinds words
to both and one man handed over his already-read
paper to the man across the aisle and one teen
sat quietly next to another sleeping on the route
and we offered seats to those more tired than us
as they stepped on and gave up spots for parents
with heavy loads, and no others would know
the beauty in those moments along our route but we
carry that love and respect for another with us
as we step off onto the paper-dotted sidewalk
that leads us to our day.

When I Say the Words

When I say the words
"I love you" to my neighbors,
to my friends,
to those I've known for years,
and to those I met
on the journey today,
I'm telling you that I see you—
The whole you…all of you.
I am not afraid of
the sight of your scars
or the sounds of your crying
or the knowledge of weaknesses…
I love the darkness of your
chocolate-colored skin
and the depth of brownness
in your soul-revealing eyes…
And I also love
the desert-kissed skin of
you, my friend, with
your deep black hair and
your chestnut-colored lips

that highlight the smile
that draws us all
into your joy…
And you with the
terra-cotta blush and
the laughter in your eyes…
And you with the
sand-colored hands
and green eyes
that disguise your mischief…
And you with the
ivory unblemished skin and blue eyes…
Or you—the one who wears your age
and shows your leathery arms
as you toil again through the day…
And you as you paint with the sunrise
or sing well past the sunset
or dance with the wind
or hum quietly as you write
or cook like your grandmother
the buttery-rich comfort food
or you—the one who adds
the spice that kicks in with each bite.
I love you

because you are like me—
You seek joy,
follow hopes,
love deeply,
daydream,
toil,
fear...
I love you
because you are different—
You sing a different song,
dance to a different beat,
create with a different style,
love in a different way,
toil using your unique gifts,
fear a different enemy…
I see you—the whole you…
And celebrate us all today…

Biding

In the moment of the memory—
that's where we belong—
in the mist that surrounds
those lingering moments between
a late -night meeting or
a connecting flight or
a two-hour conference call,
that's where we all join as one.
We reflect upon a shared meal
or an unexpected hug
or a good laugh with a friend.
And we smile as we enter
this shadowland where our
memories link us to love
and in this moment
time stands still
and waits for us to learn
that in a moment with the memory
the hurriedly forgotten becomes
the eternally beloved.

As You Sleep

I watch you, so still in
your bed, arms tucked
around snuggly bears and
giraffes, your kitten curling
around your head
on your pillow cradling your
blond swirls of hair that you
dare me to try to tame…
I wonder what fills your
dreams and what your
tomorrows will bring…
and all I can promise you
is love, my love that was
born the moment you
were conceived, when I
longed to hold you and
to know you, though no
soul can fully be known…
and I watch your tiny
feet twisting beneath
your soft purple sheets

and see your toes start
the stretch that
will move up through
your legs and arms
until those curious eyes
join the awakening and
open to greet the day…
my child, it's your day.

You Were There

You were there in the center of the room
welcoming others into the moment,
taking hands, offering hugs,
showing gratitude for their presence,
and I entered from the far back and moved to
the wall and tried to assess what I should do
on this night when I came in as unexpected
as snow on a late spring day with no plans of
what to say or how to move through the moment
with those who knew how to belong,
and you saw me as I bypassed the line for
fear of having to converse with others that
I did not know how to trust or how to
make small talk as if I understood the world
through which they moved.
And I glanced in your direction wondering
if you felt shame or joy in having to find me there,
and I feared that I had disappointed you with
an appearance from someone who
others would say, how does she dare.
But without hesitation you held out a hand

and took mine and pulled me into a hug
that spoke to the room and said you
knew my name and called me friend
and that you accepted me there in
the presence of others whose appearance
fit the scene much more than I ever could.
And your voice spoke with love and
your hands held on to mine as you
spoke my name to others and confirmed
that you accepted me as an unexpected gift
without defining me as a burden to be explained.
And in the room, I knew I was real and whole
and seen through the eyes of one who knew that
when love reaches out, hope begins and
you were there to usher it in.

From the Steps

I sit tonight and watch the city
The planes hang in the sky
waiting for the right to
once again touch the earth
The stars strain to be seen through
the glare of lights we cling to
The park is quieter now
but a jogger still pounds the pavement
and breathes deeply as if seeking hope
The bus moans past dropping off
the weary-eyed and
picking up the soon to be
The cat slinks by in pursuit of a meal
but has never tasted the fresh air
I feel the breeze and know that
this wind has also touched
the bakery down the road
I hear the cars and know that
some meetings have just ended
and some parties have just begun
Some people are searching

for a cigarette
and some are trying to
stay away from a beer
The sights and sounds and feelings
all belong to my city
and I am a part of all of this
from my spot on the steps

Your Square

I hold the folded cloth
as I promise not to cry
but know the tears are waiting
flowing deep inside

and
I hear them call your name
as others turn to see
the person stepping forward
who holds your memory,

and
I hand them a square
and receive one solitary rose
as I feel the cruelty of AIDS
that so many of us know

and
now you are part of a quilt
with your name stitched for eternity
next to the others who died
when others judged you all so harshly

and
the legacy you left behind
will live on through others and through me
because we saw you for more than the disease
that couldn't erase the beauty of the person you were
created to be

Words

I watch you struggle
to find your words
that the world demands you
speak, but I don't need the
sounds to know
what thoughts you
don't need words to say…
you speak through
your eyes and through
your smile…through your tears
and through your hugs…you
dance across the room each day
when your joy overflows
and you bend in frustration
when your sorrows take
control…you take my hand
and show me things I would
have never seen…and you
kiss me good night with a love
that will never cease…your eyes
shine with hope and your arms

hold your love…the sounds are
in your movement and your
gentle spirit breathes your song…
your life is a whisper of hope
and shout of love, my child,
so may the song go on, my love,
and let the world hear
your heart's words.

The Morning Crew

Your youthful hopes and plans for life
sat inside of you as you huddled together
outside of the McDonald's in view of the
red carpets that would be rolled out for others
and you hid your hurts and fears as you
fought for ways to survive until your worthiness
was realized by those who walked by and
you wondered how to earn their trust so
you could earn a meal and you planned together
ways to capture the elusive goals of home and health
and hope as you talked about the skills and gifts you
had to offer those of us moving past as you assumed
we never heard your whispered words and you shared
the meal dropped off at your feet in a bag because you
knew you needed each other and that the whole was
stronger than the parts and I listened without any words
of wisdom because I knew the harshness of the realities
of the world into which you wanted to move
and I knew the blindness people walked with
as they passed you on the street and I wanted to
encourage you and tell you that hopes would be

realized and dreams would come true and life
would open doors for you but those doors
were out of my reach, too, and I had no
keys to success and health and hope so I
bowed my head and offered thanks for
the only things we had—the people who stood
with us in the spots where our pain led.

Jonni's Time

I stand by your grave
hidden under the shade tree
and wonder where you'd be
if you were still here today…
I'd ask you about your life
and sunsets on the beach,
about the friends you loved and
all about your tears, and for me,
I really want to know if you
ever see my heart from
your eternal home, 'cause this
should be your time,
the time for you to live
and share more of your
heart with the one who's waiting
for just another day with you,
and I really want to know the
joys of your life
that were extinguished
way too soon, that were
dancing with you through the day

when you left before I knew all
that I wanted to know, and I want
to hear you laugh as you did
when we would play and
I want to see your grin
like when I didn't get my way.
I want your music to flow
through me once again, and
to sit with you at dusk
out of sight of the rest of
the world and tell our secrets of
our lives just once more…
please one more talk again.

faith

Walking

For those of us whose feet have walked
along a path for which we need forgiving
God offer forgiveness

For those of us whose feet have tread
upon the rights of others as we walked along our journey
God offer forgiveness

For those whose feet have travelled along a path
of fear or suffering because of the misstep of others
God offer wholeness

For those whose feet have known
a path of illness or injury
God offer healing

For those whose feet have walked beside
a friend or family member whose path led to death
God offer peace

For those whose feet have chosen
an unknown road along their journey
God offer courage…

God's Good Morning

God of the Morning
wrap me in your wonder
fill me with the morning song
hold me with the breeze

God of the Stillness
quiet my heart
and its restlessness this dawn
let me awaken with your peace

God of New Beginnings
lift me up again
help me find new strength today
let me fly with the courage of the wind

With Me

God of my past, help me to know
that when I could not cry
You shed a tear for me—
that when I could not laugh
You sat by me patiently

God of my present, help me to know
that through my loneliness I may not see them
but a host of saints surround me—
that through my sorrow I may not hear it
but all of creation calls my name

God of my future, help me to know
that through the changing paths of my life
step by step you will walk with me—
that my True Companion you will always be
and through new love and life you will strengthen me

Joining the Jubilee

Call the people from across the land
Sound the ram's horn now.
Call us to hear the voices of today—
The young, the old, the tired, the hungry,
The homeless, the lonely, the oppressed, the enslaved.
And for those voices declare this time sacred
And it shall be a jubilee for you.

Call all people to arise
Sound the ram's horn now.
Call us to see the sights of our times—
All of the struggling, all of the dying,
All of the crying children of God.
And for those visions declare this time sacred
And it shall be a jubilee for you.

Call all people to freedom
Sound the ram's horn now.
Inaugurate our search for justice—
Our search for answers pulsing through our lands.
Call us to search together hand-in-hand.
And for this searching declare this time sacred
And it shall be a jubilee for you.

Knowing God

O, God the Wise One
teach me—
I call out questions in your name
I search this morning for answers
that will help lead me on today.
O, God the Lover
touch me—
let me feel you close against me
holding me so tightly in your arms
so I will know I'm yours as you say.
O, God the Mother
nurse me—
pull me to your breast
and nourish me with your sweet milk
that will sustain me along my way.
O, God the Companion
know me—
call me by my name
and touch my hand and hold my heart
and come with me as I play.

Tragedy

Tragedy walks among us
displaying the deadly strokes
of her strength
piercing through all of our lives
Tragedy defeats the moment
but Faith keeps eternity

Last Breath

I know…
I had loved you as fully
as I knew how to love…
I know…
it was time
To say goodbye…
To end your suffering…
To release you fully
into the Hands of God.
I thought…
I was ready…
I had prepared…

But I feel…
Unsure of how to let you go…
Lost without the phone call…
Empty without your hands
reaching out to hold mine
as I search for a new path
through the grief
shadowing me now.
You were…
My memory sharer
My first best friend
My teacher
My comforter
The one who worried about me
The one who knew me from birth
The one who held my children
as tightly as you first held me
The one who was so different from me
yet still so much the same
…forever and always…

I will love you
As I journey forward
I will love you
Throughout eternity
I will carry your stories
And share your hopes
And laugh at jokes
I would have told you
And remember your words
And cherish your pictures—
The ones in frames
And the images of you in my heart.
You are loved.
You are remembered.
You are both at Home
And forever here in me.

In Celebration of Our Awakening

We awaken from our deep slumbers
arising from long winters which buried us
in sorrows and burdens that froze our soul
and in this season our spirit hibernated
out of the instinct for survival
but now we awaken and rediscover ourselves—
we find in us a child
celebrating dawn as if it were the first…
we find in us a lover
embracing all things beloved
in us and around us…
we find is us a warrior
charging forth with courage
as if no one could stand in our way…
and we discover our roots
which seek out sustenance
as they are caressed by the rich soil
through which they move
and we celebrate our new growth
as we reach up to you, Holy Mother,
and we feel your warming powers
which have awakened us this day.

Grace

Grace is having nothing and still finding joy…
Grace is being a daisy in a rose garden and still being loved by the gardener…
Grace is being slow and the race not determined by speed…
Grace is looking down and seeing the reflection of God in the pool of tears at my feet…
Grace is the parent loving the song of a child even when it is sung off key…
Grace is being covered in the mud of a mistake and still being hugged when we track our footprints through the house when we come back home…
Grace is having fear lessened through the voice of a friend…
Grace is seeing the ladybug on my daughter's hand and watching her smile…
Grace is the unconditional love and the smile at the end of our journey…
Grace is renewing our spirit…
Grace is getting a glimpse of who we can be one day…
Grace is being loved for who we are right now…
Grace is not having to understand it to have it…

Thankful for God's Ways

I bowed my head at the table
as someone read aloud and
I heard them end with
"My peace be with you"
but I didn't understand
how anyone could say that
on this very day…
think that God sent peace…
a young child ill
a grandfather gone
a mother facing life-and-death choices
my life uprooted and torn apart.
Peace in the midst of this?
Rumors and gossip swirled around
and people turned away.
I ran home and cried
from the deepest part of my soul
"How could you forsake me?"
"Why don't I have your peace?"
"How can I deal with this now?"
"What could possibly be next?"

Quietly, in the beating of my heart,
I felt the answer and
I knew that God was calling
through the tears and through the pain
"Whatever is now, I am here."
"Whatever is next, I am already there."
I stopped crying and listened
to the stillness in my soul.
My tears ceased and my fears eased
and I moved to the window
and saw the leaves moving with the soft breeze
as if beckoning to a new day.
"My peace be with you."
"Let's get on our way."
With the next meal, I bowed my head
and prayed to God and remembered
I am thankful for God's ways.

Morning

To touch upon the morning
with the restless spattering of squirrels,
the rustle of leaves from birds taking flight
and then landing and chattering with others on the wire—

To touch upon the morning
with the caress of a breeze upon my cheek,
the hug of the new grass wrapping around my feet
and the dew wandering across my skin—

To touch upon the morning
and share the day divine…

What this is about…

This is not about politics,
not parties, not platforms…
This is about people…
And possibilities…
Promises to keep…
Hope to hang on to…
This is about being loved…
And being love…
About the love that can't
be defined or controlled
by one group alone…
This is about the justice
longed for since
the most ancient of days…
About peace dreamed of…
About faith that goes beyond
human logic and beyond
my own desires and wishes—
A faith that sees humanity as a whole…
A faith that tells me to open doors
and share hope

and build homes

and shatter abuse

and feed the hungry

and drive out hate

and speak truth

and take chances

and walk on water

and break bread

and shine light

and walk away from my comfort

in order to bring about

a safe place where

all can seek faith and hope

and love and light and joy and peace

and justice and mercy

Together…

For God so loved the world…

change

The Rising

I remember the
falling and
the feeling of
failing—the
flight down
took one word
to begin and
years to finish.
Tethered by shame
and pain, I stayed
down until that
one breath—the sigh
that turned into
a whisper …
a small call to
an identity free
from the chains in
the depths of defeat—
and I listened and
I whispered more truths
before finally speaking

my own hope aloud.
And I felt myself
rise first to my knees;
then in prayerful
belief that life awaited,
I felt the pain
of muscles straining
to stand and felt the
flesh tearing as
the chains fell.
But this pain was
affirming my hopes,
and I rose to my feet
and pulled myself
from the pits of your hell,
and as the air reached
my wings, I knew
I had survived.
I rose. I flew.
I began to thrive.

A Lover's Cry

I dropped the cup.
Of all that happened that day,
that's what I remember.
I heard the sound of it
breaking on our wooden floor.
I felt the first crack move through
me, then heard each tiny piece
breaking away from the whole
and finding its way to a
final resting place.
Somewhere in the moment
my cry joined in with the
sound of the breaking.
My wail seemed separated
from me, though, as if my soul
had moved to the corner
of the room and wept from there.
That's all I remember.
I know tearful friends had arrived
and waited on our screened porch
for me to answer their hesitant knock.
I lazily moved their way with my hot tea

brewing in the mug you had given me for
my birthday as I strolled their way, not
knowing that this would be the last moment
when I expected you to be home soon.
I wonder now what my life
would have been like if I had not
answered their knock, but I know
the grief would have reached me still—
clawing its way through any wall I tried
to build around myself, digging through the floors,
or hovering above waiting to descend and break
my heart, so the news of your passing met me
at the door, I'm told, but all I remember
is dropping the cup and letting the
tea scald my feet as I stood planted
before my friends as broken as
the mug which will never again be whole.

Together...Not Against

When did it become
if...then?
When did it become
forcing me to choose
between
you
them or
me?
When did we divide
our allegiances into terms
that say if you love them,
you can't love me...
or if I speak for them
then I must not be able
to speak also for you?
Where's the us
in it together?
Where's the global humanity
that's biblical and moral and just?
Where's the understanding
that I can love them

and love you and
call people back
together as us?
Races…
Religions…
Professions…
Callings…
Identities…
By raising my voice for one,
I am not raising my voice
against another…
Hear the call that
all can be healed
all can be whole
all can have justice
all can be loved
…it's not about choosing
which people to stand with…
I'm just standing and helping all
rise up and stand…
It's together…not against

The Border of Your Land

I walked among the fallen trees,
the oaks that were decaying,
the pines that were bent over to the ground,
the pecans that lost their purpose.
I listened to the creaking and groaning
of branches breaking and
limbs falling from their mighty heights.
The blame fell on others who
had only walked paths around the
untouchable trunks that warned
them of private protected lands
and boastfully wore their signs
created to bring fear to all who
may dare tread on your sacred ground.
But you are lower now than
your resting fallen friends.
Death drug you beyond where
their bows will descend.
Children will frolic here now
and make swords of the sticks
previously out of their reach
and lovers will sit on the trunks

forming benches for their rest
and they will plan their forever here
and youth will make balance beams
on the wide remains calling to them
with a teasing hope that
they can reach new heights of glory and
attain feats you dared them to dream.
You barricaded yourself
and your self-serving beliefs
behind a fence and a line of trees
that never stopped your hate from growing
within your walls.
You missed this moment
with the laughter and the dance and the song,
with the pledge of love,
and the leap of hope.
Your name and your game are now gone.

Happy Words

I saw what you wrote

when you asked people to be quiet—

to quit talking so much about subjects

that make you uncomfortable—

that make you tired of hearing

the same thing over and over—

you want no more "me too" posts or

"black lives matter" thoughts to

cross your screen, to interrupt your comfort.

Do you need only happy words

to validate the world you created in your mind?

Is your call for silence a hope

that there is no more hate and that no more hurt

will be inflicted on another?

That bruises will fade and scars will heal

and hearts will find new hope?

Or are we calling for your world to change

in ways that makes you face those

that you have helped silence for

so many years or hear the cries that you

have pushed so far from your

thoughts that it's easier to say

they must be the ones who are wrong

rather than say, me too, I see now

a way to bring hope and life and healing…

I need to say their names and

seek their faces and listen to the pain

they cry out in streets and on ball fields

and in marches and online

and I need to see my role in the

ongoing injustices that plague our land

and destroy hope and exalt

indifference over love…

Silence will not change truth.

Indifference will not erase the need.

The tears will fall, and the voices will rise through it all…

Edges

Standing at the edge
always
I look back and face
the terror of the world left behind
or look forward and face
the terror of the unknown space ahead
Standing at the edge
always
I choose to close my eyes
and step out into what seems
like nothing but thin air and slowly
move step by step onto a delicate cloud of hope
Standing at the edge
always
I move ahead, eyes still closed,
sweat clinging to my back,
uncertainty surrounding me
and being held up only by the emptiness around

Standing at the edge
always
I open my eyes one by one
and feel a new sensation
discovering I'm standing on solid ground—
with newly found courage I flew across the chasm of the
unknown
Standing on the edge
always
I build a bridge of hope and love
and light the path for you to see
as you navigate through your own fears
and find a way over your own valley of the unknown
Standing on the edge
always
we survive
what others cannot perceive
and we cross uncharted oceans
to new worlds untouched by those who brought us to the
edge with fear
Standing on the edge of hope
always…

The Days

The days pass by so quickly
some without the joy
I thought I would always carry with me…
I try to recapture it
by hearing your voice call my name
as you did all through my childhood…
calling me for meals or church
or to remind me of a chore…
calling me to share news
or just to check in
You walk with me
even on days when we
are not together…
On days when I am closed
in an office with numbers
swirling around in a tornadic frenzy
until I gather them to their
cells on the spreadsheet before me…
You are with me when I worship…
Even when you are in a church miles away
or resting at home because
you can no longer make the trip…

You are with me on the drive to see you
in a home that will always fill my heart and
soul
with thoughts of family and meals
and prayers and time that seemed to stop
for just a moment when we laughed…
I cannot slow time
I cannot heal
But I can love
I can remember
I can live out
all that I was taught
and hold on to
all that I cherish
and pass along
the stories to
all who will listen…
And I will remember…
And I will love…

Empty Circles

I sit in the emergency room
watching doors open and close,
watching tears flow, families embrace,
people sitting alone with their pain,
and hearing whispered prayers,
angry sobs, broken hearts tell the story to a nurse
taking notes before moving on to the
next voice calling out for help,
and I wonder if I have walked past any of
these people as I rush from one
thing to another that calls to me from my calendar
and I realize that I haven't truly touched many lives
but I have walked in empty circles
that fed me the feeling of doing good
and I thought I thrived on the praise
for being a happy helper
who cut and pasted and designed and planned
and showed up for programs and shows
that made the kids smile and looked great
in my photos shared with friends
and we all pretended these had a purpose
so we ran in the empty, endless circles of service

that led us nowhere on the journey
to change the forces that defeat so many—
the hunger, the hurts, the lack of
access to hope for so many—and my
empty circles tired me though I held on
to the feeling with the illusion of
mighty works being done and my weariness
blinded me to the needs of those I walked past
to show up for the swirling of activity
and deafened me to their cries as I rushed
to fulfill another empty role leading nowhere
other than to my own desires to say I served
without ever having to grow
so I circled and swirled and praised myself
and my peers for the choice to draw
others in to the empty circles so they, too,
could pretend the movement mattered

Fears

I listen to the hushed whispers
coming from the pews behind
talking about all the new faces
filling seats and changing places …
people whose boldness is the talk of the town…
and I hear the groups of diners in our town's tiny cafe
ordering Sunday lunch and feeding others thoughts
about the newcomers sitting just three chairs down
and I can close my eyes and remember
where your words come from…
your fears are formed from falsehoods
fed to you from birth…
deceptive tales about the horrors of "those people"
who aren't like you…
images created in your mind that frame your thoughts
about who can be included in the self-created world
you work so hard to protect…
the world that chooses
favored colors and worries when shades start to blend…
a world where women are ladies and men are men…
where houses are built on the right side of the tracks
and business is done with anyone else out back…

where poverty is handed out through brutal hands,
then defined as a weakness of the ones
who refuse your commands…
where white is pure and all else tainted…
don't you dare touch or the stigma will haunt you…
where comfort comes through well-defined roles
of status and gender and race and your place…
but those fears fall apart when the walls come down
and truths about others try to step in…
and the voices of your past call out warnings to your mind…
don't you dare trust or they will steal you blind…
and the cashier at the drugstore has a unique mind
and you wish she would go back to where she
belonged in your time…
and those spoon-fed fears
continue to grow as long as you water them and
and give them room to thrive…
they are the seeds of hate that we allow to survive.

Nowhere for Love

The room is empty.
She's gone now—
her reflection isn't in the bedroom mirror;
her voice isn't calling from the other room;
no hands are reaching out for mine.
Her scent is here—
that lingering smell of lavender
from her drugstore lotion.
And when I close my eyes,
a lifetime of memories tumble through my mind…
tree trimmings and turkey,
ice cream and cakes,
hugs for comfort and for shared joys.
But my eyes are wide open now,
and my heart is aching with the wandering love
that is left inside me with no place to go,
no one to share it with…
my love…her love…
the love I felt with every phone call,
with letters written
and gifts wrapped

and meals planned
and games played
and movies watched
and joys shared
and tears hugged through.
This love that is left behind
weaves through me
with a sense of being lost,
as if it now grows inside of me
with no purpose or promise of ever being known.
This love...my love…her love…will never perish.
It will breathe inside of me until I, too, depart this earth.
But for now I have nowhere to place it—
nowhere for this love.

Really?

That small boy that you passed
sitting on the bench
waiting for the bus
that would take him
back to that place
where his eyes dim
and his heart breaks
and the little girl
who was crying in the
grocery store that you
stopped in on your way
home but where you
were busy deciding on a
quick dessert and failed
to notice her bloodied nose
(or hear the voice that said
"be good—you deserved that")
well, they wondered if you
will remember them
in your prayers that you
squeeze in before work unless
you oversleep in which case

you try to say them before you
grab dinner and a movie
and they wonder if you would
possibly find a moment to speak out
on their behalf unless you
are tired from the lecture
you gave or from balancing
your checkbook late last
night in which case they
will continue to fend for
themselves if they
survive the fight.

Secrets

I looked around this
imaginary place where
faces pretended to belong—
Could anyone know?
Can you tell? Does it show?
I don't want to be here—
to chat as if I trust or love
the people in this circle
with whom I have been thrust
as if our lives are at stake—
or maybe they are because
of this secret some of us share—
But do the others know?
Would they really care?
You created the brokenness
that's buried just out
of reach of my voice—
I never found the words
or the courage to share—

so maybe our very lives are at stake
because of the secret in this room—
because maybe we aren't still living—
becoming just a ghost of who we were
before your choices changed the
story of the lives that hide
your truths so maybe I should
cry out here—
there's secrets leading
to your doom.

Meetings

The world was still turning
as we sat locked in the room
around the large wooden table
planning meetings and receptions
arguing over details as if
they were going to change the world—
maybe try to make it spin in a new direction,
but outside the window
a woman hummed an old tune
that she remembered from her childhood
as she searched for a warm place
to rest or maybe for a bite of leftover lunch
and down the street a child
curls up on the bedroom floor
bleeding and trying not to cry
and wishing that Mom would come and hold her
yet realizing that Mom would never know
about these behind-the-door meetings
and somewhere in the city
a shot rang out in a schoolroom—
one more young man angry with the world
one more child is dying

and somewhere one teen with a belt
around the neck is taking one last breath
thinking no one would care—
no one would listen,
and back in our meeting we are still listening
only to our own voices
as if we were going to change the world.

just

me

No Such Thing

There
is
no
such
thing
as
being
too
broken
to
love.

As Time Goes By

Runners to your mark
Runners set
Go

The clock has started
Time flows by
Now

Race the elements
Chase the wind
Fly

The ground holds you back
Muscles strain
Past

The tape is broken
Time has won
Again…

Turritopsis dohrnii

Immortal they call you…
the jellyfish that just won't die…
you've outsmarted our reality
and refused to claim the
terms of others as your own
even when you are on
the dark, descending path that
leads to death and you
fall to the ocean floor
thought to be gone from this world,
you begin again from those
dark depths of supposed defeat
and then you rise and I
see your beauty,
your flowing tentacles
moving with grace through
the warm waters of your home
where few know you are present…
few care that you are alive…
the light moves
through you and with you
as you evade those who

seek you as prey and as you
defy death that follows you
so closely and calls your name…
and you call my name
and tell me to learn to rise as you
and began again a new life
with the light moving through me
and a new hope
creating a new path
as I learn again how to begin…
again and again and again…
the immortal overcomer…
let us rise again…

Unnamed Love

I never found
the words to tell you
how I felt the day
you first took my hand
and helped me up
the steep terrain
and as I reached level ground
I looked into your eyes
but I could not name
what I saw there
so I wanted to ask you
if you would
hold my hand again

and let us walk together
until we rested in the shade
of the mighty oak
and listened to the rambling stream
and there we would embrace
like lovers from a distant age
rediscovering the passion that
found its way to this lifetime
and met us on our path
but my longings went unnamed
and we talked of things that
are unremembered now and
I wait to find my words—

Musician

Did you know
I was hiding on the steps
last night
waiting for your magic?
And suddenly it came
willowing through
my evening dreams,
wandering through my soul.
You carried me
by music to a land beyond
my reach and you lifted me
with laughter
as your fingers
stroked the keys
and from my
hiding place I leapt
and I danced across
the moon as your magic
carried me
and you made my
nighttime sing.

Cinquain

Colors
Creeping through the
Crevices of the sky,
Smiling through the seraphic tears--
Rainbows

Golden
Rays flowing from
The skies curing someone's
Sorrows and drying someone's tears--
Sunshine

Redefining Now
(For a Sweet Friend)

I sit at my table where I see the Christmas cactus
creeping over the edge of the shelf
after waiting to bloom when the new year has begun
and I know what most of my tomorrow holds—
I will sit at my desk and follow
the familiar patterns of life so
well defined by expectations of others
who tackle the same challenges every day—
there will be the times of day when I pray
knowing others of my faith do the same—
the times when I send a quick text to
my daughter or follow up on a promise
with my son or meet for dinner with the love
of my life and share our thoughts of the day—
but here at my table I must redefine now—
this moment that should have been yours—
when I would call to ease my worries,
checking in on the one who for years
had to check in on me—
when I would promise you that I would see you soon

for what had become the familiar
moments of our shared times—
plans that connected our now to our tomorrow—
and this moment in my kitchen should have been ours still,
a time when I dropped my purse and keys on the table,
done with the details of my day, and I reached for the
phone knowing you would be there waiting for me,
calling so I could hear your voice and
 know that you heard mine
and we would talk about our next hellos and
not quite yet about our goodbyes—
and so I shed a tear and seek a hug and
try so hard to feel you near because,
Dear Mom, I love you, and now is
when I wish you were here.

The Sounds

The sounds of the words of hate
came first—
the name calling
the threats both aloud and
whispered to a passerby…
Then it was the fighting
in the streets—
the fist fights among
different groups
then knives
then guns…
Then it became real,
turning hate into a war—
winner keeps all…
The shelling came next…
the bombs rocked our houses
and our schools and places of worship…
No place was safe…

Then came the cries of children
and mothers calling out the names
of children who would
never answer again…
and husbands and brothers and
and wives and sisters
and best friends and lovers…
Then the weeping before
the enormity of our pain
devoured our ability
to feel much less grieve…
So there was silence
as if we were already dead—
dead to those who claimed victory,
worthless to those who didn't want
to touch our wounds or
caress our shoulders weighted
with unimaginable memories
of the sounds of the places we left—
the places we once called home…

Only Words

I forgot to tell you
that I noticed that
your eyes were not
dancing when I saw
you leaning over the
griddle dripping pancake
batter onto the hot surface
and your mind seemed
a million miles away as
you looked up and noticed
me there and you hugged me
as if I were not made of flesh
and you whispered words that
sounded like "I love you"
but they fell onto the
surface of the griddle
before they reached my ear
and they sizzled
with the batter but
you didn't seem to care

and I was looking for
the right words to say,
words that would make it to
your place of hurt inside,
but I got distracted and
you already were and I
just forgot to pick back up
"I love you"
off the griddle
and devour the words
for my sustenance for the day
and I forgot to come back
and search again for
the right words to say.

Our Lunch

I remember that day
in the car when
we were coming back
from getting lunch
and we were full
from the burgers that
had melted cheese dripping
down the side and we
were full from the
chocolate pie we split
and we were warming
our hands by the vents
on the dash of your car
when you looked over
at me and smiled and
I felt a warmth rush
through me that could not be
matched by any artificial
heat and I felt myself
blush and not know
quite what to say but
you put me at ease

by your words that
I felt surround me
but could not quite hear
over the beating of my
heart and you reached
out and took my hand
and held it in yours
and continued to chatter
casually about the day
as your eyes occasionally
met mine to catch my
response and I smiled
back and promised myself
that I would never forget
that day.

Pie in the Sky

When the cows come knocking
at your front door
And you hear your mother's voice
saying, "I'll buy three more."
When you hear a loud whir
And see a cloud fly by,
you know you've been dreaming
after eating blackberry pie.
So don't you worry—just sleep tight
and don't eat dessert tomorrow night.

Rainy Day Footprints

The beautiful tears
that are falling from heaven
quench our thirsty souls

The young bird fallen
must discover its spirit
and take flight or die

The dolphins swimming
arrive with grace and beauty
just out of my reach

The ocean calls me
and will bring me face to face
with power and peace

Listening

Under the redbud tree

we met—

You came to me in the breeze

and I felt you there

and I heard you sigh—

with a gentle patience

you waited for me

to find my words—

you stood next to the trunk,

the heart of the tree,

as if now you could touch its soul.

And you listened to my rambling

but I stopped and our eyes met

and then I knew

you listened deep inside of me,

past the actual words and my intonation.

You heard my soul, my voice

with which I longed to speak—

And you smiled at me

under the redbud tree.

Memory Box

I thought of you today
when I was unpacking
a box of things that
you sent to me for
Christmas and the
scent of you floated
from it as I tore through
the tape and I thought
of the cocoa butter soap
you wash your hands in
and the bath gel that
smells like the flowers
from the field back home
and the lotion that you
rub on your arms after
you wash the dishes and

the smell of the dinner
you just served on the
table you got while you
were married that you
now keep decorated with a
vase of flowers in the center
and a candle on each
side except when we
kids were gathered around
to play games and then
you moved everything
to the kitchen but you
carefully replaced them when
we were done and I set
the box aside for now
and went to thumb through a
photo album so I could
see your face while the
scent of you lingered around.

For Five

Dance a jig
My little one
Swirl your way through life
Laugh
And jump
And sing your song
And I will cry your tears
Chase the butterfly by day
And the firefly by night
And cuddle with kittens
And giggle with puppy's love
Find the lucky clover
And wish upon a star
And leave nightmares behind
Know how much I love you
As you dance across the sky
My little one, be happy
My little one, forever five

What Floor?

I started at the bottom,
but then I learned to climb.
Along with climbing I learned to fall,
but I learned to get back up.
Well, I'm still climbing and learning—
my friends say I'll reach the top,
but how will I know when I get there?
How high is the top?

To the Moon

I see you
luring me to the window
with your beams sent drifting
through the might—
And I do come closer
wanting to touch you
and to capture some of your mystery.
But you are only flirting with me
as you stay hidden in the fingers of the trees
or clothed in a cloud's delight.
Knowing that, I still draw near
with lingering thoughts of nights gone by,
and with a sigh I send to you
sweet dreams, dear moon, sweet dreams…

Longings

I long to call your name
but I am silent
and though I love you
the words remain unclaimed

I am silent
though I fear you
the words remain unclaimed
though I long to name you

Though I fear you
I want to understand you
though I long to name you
I must let you choose your words

I want to understand you
But you are silent
so I wait for you to choose your words
so you will long to love me

The Waiting

I don't remember what I was waiting for—
maybe I was waiting for
hearts to open,
eyes to see,
ears to hear …
maybe hope to appear,
love to grow and flow over
these dividing walls.
But I know I was waiting on others …
And I waited until I felt the air begin to chill
and until I saw the sky darken.
Hope was fading with the light.
I stood to touch a feather falling without a purpose,
waiting to see if I could hold on to the feeling of
it's flight to me.
But as I stepped forward,
I felt a new hope—
a chance to leave this waiting place
and journey forward to find my own flight,
my own purpose—
to plant the love I was waiting to grow—

to open my own eyes
to the beauty of the world
I had ignored while I waited—
to hear the hopes in the songs
that I had tuned out through my own indifference.
I stepped out of the shadows
and walked
and danced
and sang
and loved
and felt more alive
and wondered why
I was ever
waiting for you.

The Dreams Run Deep

Billowing over rocks and
surging through soil that
past generations failed to tame,
my heart leads forth like a mountain stream
with mighty strength, I claim my path
and let my soul flow free
pursuing the deepest of dreams

Let's Make Soup

Stop pouring the milk
    into the bathtub
 the babysitter yelled to the kids
And please come help me
        make your supper
You pour in the water
      You put in the potatoes
You put in three spoons of this spice
And…no, don't get the water
     out of the dog's bowl
        Wait, you put in potatoes
        not peelings
Oh, I said three spoons OF spice
   not three spoons AND spice
And we ate sterling silver spoon soup.

Look and See

To the one whose heart
becomes the eye
for the soul
nature's mysteries unfold
and are seen

Nana's Song

you taught me how to fly high
to let go of my soul
and let it reach the sky
so I'm on my way—I'm standing tall
because your love built the ladder
that lets me climb without fearing the fall

Wait for Me

Perk the eggs
fry the coffee
boil the bacon
hold that bus,
I'm coming.

Wake the kids
find the shoe
match the clothes
hold that bus,
I'm coming.

Take the books
sign the note
search for keys
catch that bus,
I'm late.

in the end

in the end
there is still love
because it will
outlast
hate and greed
anger and jealousy
so
know
that
you
are
loved
i love
and i am loved

Made in the USA
Columbia, SC
20 June 2019